BLESSINGS OF WORDS

THE BEST GIFT EVER...THE MOST ASTOUNDING BLESSING.

SUNAINA PRADHAN

Contents

Preface

The book "BLESSINGS OF WORDS" is basically a poetry book. It consists of poems of a variety of genres and categories. The author chose such a title for the book because she felt that she was very fortunate to be able to understand the beauty of words and was blessed by the words. The poet writes a variety of poems based on her own emotions. She tries her best to describe one's state of mind and heart, one's emotions using words. The poet is a nature-lover and you will be able to find some or the other element of nature in most of her poems. She says that she doesn't write for others ; rather she writes for herself and chooses to share it with others.

A Note From The Author:-

In my opinion, a writer doesn't write for his/her readers ; a writer always writes for oneself. They write because they enjoy it and then they choose to publish in order to let others feel the joy that they felt while writing down their thoughts. A poem, a story whether fictional or non-fictional, a self-help book or anything written by a writer is not just a piece of writing; it is a feeling. The writer feels every word that he has written. Writing a book doesn't just mean looking up lots and lots of dictionaries to find new words to make their writing more interesting and cut a dash; that's just the superficial part of it. The real sense of writing a book is to feel it. According to my personal and short experience, a writer feels every kind of emotion before presenting it in the form of words. Even if they haven't felt an emotion or a feeling naturally, they still try to feel and understand that emotion by putting themselves in other's shoes and analysing the situation.

And every writer including me expects only one thing from the readers and that is that the readers try to understand the emotion behind a piece of writing rather than just reading the words printed on a paper. One's personal opinion, critical thinking or critical analysis or whatever you call it is necessary; especially while reading a poem; but the true beauty of reading a poem is to see it from the poet's perspective.

I hope you will enjoy reading this book!!

-SUNAINA PRADHAN

1. THE VOICE OF SILENCE

Not everyone understands the beauty of solitude and not everyone hears to what silence speaks. Silence is everywhere and we all have enjoyed it at some point of our lives. 'Enjoyed' in the sense 'felt good and peaceful'. There are times when we are left all alone and we feel stuck and according to many people of this so-called modernistic and socialistic generation, it literally sucks. But, have you ever wondered how those saints meditating for years in solitude are so happy and calm, it feels as if they have got everything in the world. Especially in my country, India, afterall it is the land of religion, culture and saints. It is because they have realised the power of silence, they have heard the loudest version of it. And look at people around you, they are immersed and lost in the world called 'social media'. And in this world of social media, people smile and post selfies, pictures with family to show that they have a warm and happy family, but do you think they are really happy? When you sit at the table to eat, you just click pictures and post and then lose the amazing moment by getting lost in the comments firing faster than a gun fires a bullet. At the very moment, you read comments describing the flavour of the food but you surely just ate the food, you didn't taste it, you didn't enjoy the flavours. And you call SOCIAL MEDIA a stress-buster? You describe this feeling as 'happiness'? Try to listen to silence, it really has a lot to say. These days, people say that silence scares them. Tell me one thing, how can such a beautiful thing scare you? Try to feel silence, try to live it, try to enjoy it... it's right in your mind, it's in you.

In this world filled with different kinds of disturbing noises, I try to hear that one pleasant voice,"THE VOICE OF SILENCE."

THE VOICE OF SILENCE

Unchaperoned in my domicile; I was seated,
My mind was filled with thoughts and hunches unimpeded;
I was slouching around my humble abode,
Calm and hushed; all composed!

The alluring moon was in full bloom,
The moonlight invaded my infinitesimal room;
A voice creeped into my ears,
Keeping aside all my fears;
Conscientiously I'd try to hear;

"You are with the best soul ever", Silence spoke to me.
"Who is it ?"
"Today I enounce,
And you must hear!
I'm Silence,
The loudest among all;
When there's no one,
Into your mind I'll crawl;
When you leave the human world,
I'll be the only one you can call;
I can give you peace,

I can bring back memories,
Whether merry or sad,
Whether good or bad,
I can do things beyond your imagination,
I'll be you final destination.

You'll weep in silence,
You'll rejoice in silence,
You'll embrace THE SILENCE;
You'll become THE SILENCE one day,
When you will leave you, to your dismay!

I'm the one who leads you to sleep,
In your mind, it's me that you keep;
Your lips are sealed,
And then I speak,
You keep things concealed,
And I'm quite sleek,
I know you,
And today you know me.
I'm Silence, the attire that you put on everyday.

-Sunaina

2. THE MAGICAL BOOK

WHAT IS A BOOK?...Everyone's got different answers. That definition freak would say,"A Book is a set of pages in which a person portrays information about any particular topic or writes his opinions.." and so on. Someone else would say,"A Book is one's true friend" and likewise, we can get a variety of answers from different people with different mindsets. By the same token, I would say,"A Book means 'MAGIC' ; it itself is 'MAGIC'." A book is a magical gift that you can open again and again, as many times as you wish to, as many times as you want to, as many times as you feel like opening it and cherishing it. What does a book basically have in it? Of course, the only answer to it is 'words'. And one amazing and magical thing that a book does is that 'when you can't express something in words, you can look for books and find words in the books' ; because some or the other writer must have explained that feeling in words which you consider unexplainable by words.

Do you know that magical and 'out of the world' feeling that one feels when one reads a book with all their heart, mind and soul? It's not just a feeling, it becomes a beautiful experience. It rekindles your imagination . You can travel to different worlds everytime you read a book. That's the thing about books; they let you travel without moving your feet. A book is like a dream that you can hold in your hands. Every book has it's own fragrance and you just have to draw the fragrance deep inside you and believe me that would be enough to make you happy. A writer and a reader are incomplete without each other and some people are both reader and writer at the same time and the good thing is that readers and writers explore a lot of lives before they die.

The only thing that can replace a book is - "The next book." Books are the plane, the train, the road; they are the journey as well as the destination. 'Books are a uniquely portable magic.' I realised that magic too and here I write, "THE MAGICAL BOOK."

THE MAGICAL BOOK

On a fine evening,
I opened a book;
The pages were blank,
And my brain shook;
"How can this be magical!
There's nothing written in it!!'

Beside the book, lay a pen,
I picked it up and put it down again and again;
Suddenly something just popped into my head,
"Write it down", the pen said;

I started writing,
The next minute,
I started thinking,
Then the next minute,
I still kept thinking,
And so, the wheel of thinking and writing started spinning!

I thought,'Enough for the day I had worked,'
In my bed, for the next Sun, I lurked;

Again the next evening,

When I openend the book,
Into the pages, I'd look,
And guess what! - It was magical;
It took me to a peculiar yet beautiful world,
I could see and feel all that I wrote.

~Sunaina

3. OH PAIN!!! {Part-I}

The title seems quite depressing, right?

I know the poem might overall give you an extremely negative impression but that's human nature. In my point of view, negative thought is the default setting of homo sapiens. 'Think positive, be positive' etc., are good as quotes and we must act in accordance with the above mentioned phrases. But look back and notice, everytime something happens, the first thing that comes to mind is a negative hypothesis or assumption and later, like just in a matter of seconds, we convince our mind to think positive and hope for the good. For instance, when something occurs to someone who is very dear to us, and we get to know about them, the first thing that we think of is what if something bad happened and quickly we start telling ourselves to think positive. So, the human mind is wonted negative.

We all feel low at times and most of us almost feel like giving up. But at the same time, the striking thought of holding on for a little longer can be felt in our bones. Sometimes, life starts to seem like a complete mess, because some irksome, odious and vexatious incidents happen concomitantly and our head is filled with the thoughts of extreme negativity that our life is being ruled by pain. I too had several incidents, a lot many moments in my life when I felt like being tortured by pain. And at times I felt low, all I could rely on to bridle my emotions were words, so I wrote to keep myselves calm, to keep holding on. We all have felt that one thing, "Am I the only one who is being tormented to such an extent by pain?" But believe me , it's not just you, everyone's got their own troubles maybe your trouble is a piece of cake for them and so is theirs to you. It absolutely okay to feel low, to feel depressed when life treats you bad but the incumbent action to be done by you is to keep fighting!!

I was frustrated because of everything happening around me and I question pain if it would allow me to cherish , thereby I write, "OH PAIN!!"

OH PAIN!!! {Part-I}

Oh Pain,
You have tortured enough,
And I have had enough;
You have hurt enough,
And I have fought enough;
You have killed enough,
And I have survived enough;
You have given enough,
And I have put up with you enough;
You have broken me enough,
And I have built myself enough;

Isn't that enough????

I have cried enough,
And you've laughed at me enough;
I have tried enough,
You've relished enough;
I have begged you enough,
And you've mocked me enough;
I have pleaded you enough,
You've tormented me enough;

Oh pain!! You've been with me all the time,
Is leaving me alone in peace a crime?

Oh dear pain,
Please don't come back again;

Oh pain!! I don't need you now,
I want to cherish, would you please allow?

~Sunaina.

4. OH PAIN!!! {Part-II}

As the title suggests, this is the second part of the previous poem, 'Oh Pain!!.' This one is an absolute contrast to the previous part. Some people will find it confusing, some will think it's complicated and sophisticated. But I wrote what I actually felt. At the worst times of my life, I feel really exhausted to fight back but later when everything gets fine and returns to normal, I realise how much pain has helped me. It has made me stronger than ever, it has given me the courage to face even the worst of my nightmares with open eyes, it taught me that happiness is not something I need to wait for, I have to find my own happiness, I have to hunt for it and so have you. It's true indeed, if we never felt the pain, if we never had any sorrow or any stress or any such depressing thing, then how could we ever realise the value of happiness, how could we enjoy the happiness, how could we treasure our smile, how could we understand the joy of seeing a smile on the faces of our loved ones. It can be difficult but you have to learn to be happy, no matter what! I know, some of you might be thinking that all such things are really easy to say and not to do. You're thinking right too, it's not easy; I know it too but we all can try at least. People say forget the bad memories, forget all the depressing moments of your past and move on; believe me, I would never say so. You really don't have to forget your past, not a single moment, may that be happy or sad, because those moments of your life have made you who you are in your present. You should carry your pain and your struggle and those bad days, those scary nightmares but just don't let these things drag you back into the sea of darkness where you can't help but drown; you have to carry it in your mind and make yourself realise that everything was worth it. Smiling through pain is an art that is not known to everyone. And once you learn to smile through your pain, you're gonna be the bravest version of yourself. It won't be easy, but everything's possible as long as you keep trying.

I somehow feel thankful to pain in the end for having made me stronger and better than ever and thereby I write 'OH PAIN!!'

OH PAIN!!! {Part-II}

Oh pain!.oh my bestest friend,
All I want, is to thank you in the end;

If it hadn't been for you,
I wouldn't have been among the very few,

Who know the art of smiling through the pain,
Who try to hold themselves together over and over again;

Oh pain, you might break me inside,
But everytime, I grow harder on the outside;

If it hadn't been for you,
I would be waiting at the end of the queue,
Where people keep standing to find happiness,
But return with hands so empty and faces filled with sadness;

You taught me that I don't have to wait for happiness to come to me,
Rather I need to find happiness, no matter wherever I'll be;
Now you see,
Albeit I'm not, I'm still happy;;

Pretending that everything's alright,
It's like you and your mind in a deadly fight,

Yes, it hurts and yes it's hard,
But remember who you are;
You are the one whom pain has blessed,
You are the one who has smiled despite of being distressed .

~Sunaina

5. WINTER

I being a native of India, living in a tropical monsoon climate, love winter. Most people here would say that their favourite season is winter. Among all the existing seasons on the planet Earth, I find winter the most soothing, tranquilizing and soporific one. You know the best feeling in winter is to sleep in warm and cozy blankets and sheets and eat some hot steaming food. Winter outings and trips are amazing too but the pleasure of sleeping till late hours in the morning is something offbeat. But from my personal experience, I figured out there's something more startling in the winter and that is the morning. It will take great effort to wake up early in the winter mornings, but once you do that and step out of your door, everything will be worth it. The views that you'll see wil be remarkable. And who doesn't wait for christmas and the upcoming new year!! It was christmas, and I thought of writing something. And as I was floating all across my mind, I thought to write something about 'WINTER.'.

WINTER

The beauty of winter is something very pleasant,
But as most other things, it's transient.

The serene mornings,
When the bird sings;
The most beautiful music to a pair of ears so keen,
For those anxious eyes, a beautiful scene;

Fog and dew drops are like cherry on cake,
And like always, one's day they make;
Spider webs on bushes and grasses,
Can be seen as clear and shiny as glasses;

It's Christmas today,
For Uncle Santa, please make way;
May you be gifted what you want,
For breakfast, you can enjoy a croissant;!

The winter break is here,
Soon, it'll be a new year;
New things to do,
And dreams to pursue.

-Sunaina

6. THINK

'Think'- as soon as you hear that word, you surely start thinking something. I was just wondering and trying to write something about childhood, and then when I reflected back on my childhood, I found some stupefying moments which I guess are common for each one of us and are some of the most amazing memories which we usually do not recall. Childhood is the best stage in any human's life. Children have hearts so pure and minds so clear like the fresh stream water just formed when the beam of light touches and caresses the snow(glaciers). The first time we cry, the first time we say a word, the first step that we take and almost every other thing that we do for the very first time makes the people around us happy. It's not just that parents make children, it's the children who promote a couple from 'just a couple' to 'parents.' Take some time out and think of your childhood and I can assure you that you are gonna laugh or smile at least. Those silly things we did, the way we trusted everything that others said makes me feel so stupid and funny now. But that's

what childhood is all about. Childhood is an entire gold mine of innocence and purity. A child's heart, mind and soul are unimpeachable, they are unaware of the viruses like human-greed, anger, violence and other fatal brain-eaters. But in this crowded Earth, as we grow into adolescents and then adults, we slowly lose that innocence without even being aware about it. We get lost in working for others and often lose our happiness. A very few who choose to do what they love are content. Some people live their life to the fullest and their faces always glow with glee.

I suddenly realized that many of us have forgotten to live our life because of some mere worldly things. We care about what other people think of us which we never did as kids. When we were small, we did everything that gave us joy, that made us happy without giving a shit about what others will think. Let's try to be the same again and let us learn to love ourselves once again. I had all these thoughts on a blank and bright day. Randomly thinking of my childhood, I wrote this poem 'THINK.' And don't just turn the page after reading it once, sit with a calm mind and think...

THINK

Think of the day when you first said papa and maa,
Angel was your mum and superhero paa!
Hearing that word your mom was glad,
And your superhero became stronger because he was now a dad!

Think of the day when you first went to school..
Maybe you cried, but I went with a smile and I looked super cool,
When you returned home, mom checked your tiffin box,
And she always asked you to keep things in order,since you threw your socks;

They did so much to make you laugh, even carried you on their back,
Sometimes,they were strict in order to keep you on the right track;
You were stress-free back then,
And you grew up, not knowing when!

Everytime you fell, you cried but you stood back up again,
Your cute face was enough for you to sustain;
Those days were pretty good,
You would surely go back if you could.

Now life is difficult,
Because you're so-called an adult,
Now, for everything you need to show some result,
And when you don't understand what to do, mom and dad are the best to consult.

Life goes on, you don't have to mind,
Not just to others but to yourself too;you have to be kind;

You can't always be perfect,
You can't always be correct;
You cannot be flawless,
Because everyone in this world is a beautiful mess;

Live your life the way you wish to,
Nobody knows what others are upto,
So be yourself,
And love yourself.

-Sunaina

7. AS LONG AS YOU WANT

Our mind has the power to do almost every possible thing. We can do anything as long as we want to. In today's generation, happiness is something that most people long for but they ususally fail to understand that it is all in their hands. You can be happy as long as you actually want to be.

Just a short, little, casual poem- 'AS LONG AS YOU WANT.'

AS LONG AS YOU WANT

Life will be fun,
As long as you want it to be;
Life will be as bright as sun,
As long as you want it to be;

Life is not what makes you,
It's you who makes your life;
In this world there are very few,
Who know how to cook their troubles into a stew!

Life will be as tranquil as breeze,
And all your troubles will freeze,
As long as you keep smiling ,no matter what;
Despite of knowing, most of these mere humans just don't do that.

Just smile at your life,
It will surely smile back at you,
Just choose a pool of happiness and joy to dive,
You'll look young even if you're ninety-five.
Afterall, smiling doesn't cost you a million dollars!!

-Sunaina

8. DON'T FORGET

We often forget to think about ourselves because we are much indulged in worldly-affairs and thinking about what others think of us. We are so busy working and serving as servants that we barely have some time in the day for ourselves. Life is something that is to be lived and not won. You can never win over life, all you can do is to live it sprightly. We forget ourselves and sometimes even our dreams and chase money. We are so busy impressing others and making them feel contented that we forget about our happiness, our smiles and laughters. And I don't want you to forget that!

You were never alone, you are not alone and you will never be alone because you have always been there for yourself and please don't lose yourself to this world. A short reminder-"DON'T FORGET."

DON'T FORGET

Don't forget that you too are a human,
Not a bot, who can endlessly run;
Don't forget that life is precisely a precious one,
And not a race to be won.

Don't forget that time is precious,
Please don't waste it; being reckless;
Don't forget that life is always stupendous,
You don't have to indulge in anyone else's business;

Don't forget that you are made of flesh & blood.., not stone,
Remember that you've never been alone;
There was someone who always stood with you,
And that was none but you.

~Sunaina

9. SEE ALONGSIDE THE SEA

Soon after we hear the word 'sea', the thing that comes to our mind is a whole new world, an entire universe, something vast and something filled with wonders. When I was small, I mean, a little more younger than I am now, I used to take my cycle and go riding for some 15 kilometres or so; the journey was beautiful and so was the destination. The sea-side was really alluring and hypnotizing, the sand was filled with verbenas of different colours and the best thing was that there was absolute peace. I don't know if the journey and the destination are still as beautiful as they were because it's been years since I went there and humans won't let it stay the same. Back then, I used to park my cycle at a distance and sat close to where the waves hit the shore, I used to stare into the distant horizon and it felt amazing. No matter how bad my day would have been, that half of an evening hour always made me smile. Different shades of green and blue in the rising waves and strong, salty winds sticking to your skin , those moments are worth being treasured.

Just a miniature poem, some random words arranged beautifully-"SEE ALONGSIDE THE SEA."

SEE ALONGSIDE THE SEA

Looking at the Sun setting down;
A pretty smile took place of a frown;
Sitting at the edge of the town,
And laughing as hard as a clown;

Sitting alongside the sea,
With the one who's perfect for me,
And guess who's that?...it's meee!!
There's lot much to see,
Along with a cup of coffee...
alongside the sea.

-Sunaina

10. I FELT...

'Feelings'- this simple eight-lettered word is probably the most complicated one in human mind. Every minute, every second, every moment , every now and then in our life ; we keep feeling something. My love for nature can never be less. It makes me feel so amazing. When the sky is filled with grey clouds, it brings back memories to me, often sad ones as if even I would have a downpour like clouds. When there are brown clouds in the sky, it makes me feel the pain that nature feels because of air pollution caused by human activities. When the first raindrop of monsoon falls on me, it makes me feel the freshness of nature, the breathtaking views around me make me feel the beauty in every element of nature. When the raindrop just rolls down over my skin and falls on the newly formed soil and on the soft green grass fields, I can feel the sweet aroma of soil softly tingling the senses in my nose, and running into my rushing blood reminding of how the seedlings will very soon grow into a beautiful green field and then ripe slowly changing into a beautiful golden yellow just

as the morning sun shines among the clouds and it becomes a ray of hope for the farmers. They can already make me feel the happiness that the farmer would feel seeing the bits of gold turning into beautifully engranved ornamental jewellery. The storm can make me feel the rage of nature. When the winds touch me and pass by, they carry away all my stress away from my mind, away from me to the distant horizon. Nature has made me feel almost every existing feeling.And not only I felt nature, but it has felt me too.

Sitting in my backyard at night, I just wrote what I felt at that moment. And a simple title -"I FELT...".

I FELT...

Sitting under a tree,
Late at night;
Right above me,
The most beautiful sight;

Bracing breezes blowing,
Zillions of stars are glowing,
Feels like the trees are prattling,
Convictions in my mind are no longer battling;

I feel so free tonight,
I feel the nature consoling me,
I feel the winds running through me,
I feel the stars encouraging me,
I can feel the love,
I can feel the trust,
I feel honesty and loyalty...
In the winds,the trees, the sky, the stars..in THE NATURE and in ME.
All my stress just flew away,
For happiness, I have made way,
And here I say,
Nature feels you,
Nature heals you.
-Sunaina

11. DO YOU REMEMBER ??

The covid-19 pandemic changed our lives drastically. People who always stayed out of their houses were also locked up in their own houses. It was something that the world had not seen in years. For some people, the lockdown was boring; for some, devastating and for some, it was like a boon. There have been both positive and negative sides to it. It taught us basic hygiene once again, it gave us time to learn dozens of new things; some learned to cook, some learned music, some read their subjects, some did extra work from home and lot of other stuff. There have been negative effects too which I would not bother talking about. But me as a student , seeing from the view of most other students, realized how much our lives had changed!! We studied on smartphones, desktops, laptops and other gadgets for almost two whole years. We missed sitting with our friends and teachers, learning and having fun together, but we still made it through.

I suddenly came across some thoughts about how my life as a student changed. Looking at it from the perspective of all students, I write this poem-'DO YOU REMEMBER??' which talks about all those things that we enjoyed at school.

DO YOU REMEMBER ??

Do you remember how life was years back ?
You used to go to school galloping with a hefty backpack;
You went hell for leather on the cloister,
On the day of practicals, your eyes had a quirky luster!

Scrutinize how life has transmuted,
Right in our houses, we are all rooted;
The classroom where you could never be unobstrusively seated,
And now in the same class virtually, you are mostly muted!

There were days with your besties where you'd laugh raucously,
And no one could figure out the reason even after examining scrupulously;
Among your friends,you'd exaggerate your despondency,
They'd remind you that in their lives, you're an exigency;

Those wonderful days back at school were filled with glee,
I know you too are like a cat on a hot tin roof waiting for the virus to flee;

Teachers didn't just sit with you to elucidate lessons,
To perk you up, they even conducted some laughter sessions;

Yeah, I know you miss those days just like every other student,
We were all so fortunate to have spent time with teachers so prudent;
Yes indeed, sometimes they were stern,
Some chapters quaked our brains like a butter churn;
However, they always tried to turn our worst nightmares into our greatest mights;
The right one was always vindicated no matter how knotty were the fights!

Everytime we heard our principal's disquisition,
It was like our brain was undergoing fission;
Yes we all miss that school-stuff,
On the sports ground, we were exceptionally tough;

An enormously tiny virus emerged,
To stay incarcerated in our houses, everyone urged;
Technology and our lives then completely merged,
Unduly stress came on over our heads and perched;

Let's hope, our lives return to normal,
Once again, we get to put on a livery so formal;
And have the fortune of fraternizing with our mentors and friends,
To you, zillions of well wishes your bosom friend sends.
Stay strong and have a positive hunch,

In order to be unsusceptible to stress, take a healthy lunch.

Have fun ,
Because very soon you'll have to wake up before the sun;
And rush to the place you miss the most,
Because at school, you're not a guest but a host!!

~Sunaina

12. INDIAN FOOD

Food can lift the worst of moods. I love food, especially those very famous, native and traditional ones. Food, especially in my country is extremely delicious. India is a land of diversity, which means different people with different tastes, a wide range of culture and traditions and a lot of amazing dishes. And another amazing thing is that no matter which corner of the country you visit, there's one popular line that you'll hear, 'Atithi Deva Bhava'; which means that guests are equivalent to gods. And trust me, no matter how big a villa you go to or how small a hut you visit, you will always be welcomed with warmth and compassion; moreover you can't escape without eating, no one's going to care how full your stomach is, they'll still feed you with all that they have; simple yet exquisite. You'll love the astounding combination of different spices, varities of aroma, blast of flavours and all of this in a single plate. Every state, every town, every city has got it's own speciality. You can't leave India without having Indian food. Not just veggies and meat, not just salt and pepper, not just fries and curries, not just sweets and desserts, not just snacks, not just tea and beverage, not just salads and sandwiches, not just sauce and salsa, not just achar and papad (pickle and crisps), not just food, you'll be served lots of love dissolved in everything. And here, the best chef is mom and other family members as well; home-made food and mom-made food always taste best. Even the simplest of meal served with love and affection will taste amazing.

Here's a poem about the amazing food of my country, India - "INDIAN FOOD" and all the dishes mentioned in it are a must to try. I surely couldn't find space to write about every dish, it's going to be an infinite list.

INDIAN FOOD

Unquestionably, international cuisines are good,
But there's something exceptional about Indian food.

The stupefying amalgamation of spices,
That can rekindle your taste buds;
Succulent are tossed crabs pulled straight out of the muds,
Indians prefer large chunks of meat rather than slices;

The most appetizing breakfast is 'Aloo ka Paratha with desi ghee',
Eat it with chilled yogurt and all your worries will flee;
In Southern India, nothing can beat the combination of 'Idli and Sambar',
And yes! As always, coconut chutney is the star.

We have baked pastry with savory filling called 'Samosa',
How about trying out some 'Masala Dosa';
On every holy occasion, people eat 'Halwa Puri',
The festival of colours HOLI is incomplete without ' Gujiya and Kachori',

If you ever visit India,
Don't forget the snacks,
Be quite cautious,

Because the food is extremely delicious,
Don't forget to try,
Our signature 'Masala Chai'.

Our land is famous for desserts and sweets,
No matter what day it is,
Only with a sweet, every meal will finish,
We have,
'Rosogolla', 'Gulab-jamun',
'Pedha and barfi',
Even in these, we have lots and lots of variety!!

If you come to my home country,
No matter which state you're in;
You'll be treated like God,
Because the rule is 'Atithi Deva Bhava';
You will be stuffed with food,
And the food will be amazingly good!!!

-Sunaina

13. THE MOON AND IT'S LEGEND

The moon symbolizes eternity because of which it is often related to love, it signifies progress and immortality. The moon usually represents a cycle or a phase and if i was asked what I think about it, then I would say that the moon actually depicts human life. There always comes a day when moon doesn't show up in the sky which we either call as new moon or no moon and I personally find these two contrasting words absolutely correct. When the moon doesn't appear in the sky, the night sky is left dark, the moonlight is missing which is similar to the dark moments in our life, when we feel low and depressed and drained out and at the same time, it also symbolizes the beginning of a new journey; because we all know there would be no happiness in our lives if we never had sorrow in our life, thereby it also signifies the awe-inspiring ingress of euphoria in our lives, so calling it a new moon also would not be wrong. The crescent and gibbous moon then signify the growing happiness, the journey which we go through and then finally the full moon would depict the accomplishment of our task, achievement of goal, and insurmountable gaiety.

Mythology has never failed to enchant me and draw my heed to it. And after gathering some information, I found some flabbergasting tales about the moon and thereby I write -"THE MOON AND IT'S LEGEND."

THE MOON AND IT'S LEGEND

Sitting under the sky, watching the moon tonight,
Full in shape and full of light;

Very few people adore the moon and the stars these days,
Because street lights have filled all streets and ways;
Just turn off all the artificial glow-worms,
(Anyways, they'll be gone in case of severe storms);

Move to the highest place of where you live, maybe a cupola,
I'd prefer a cup of hot coffee rather than cola;
Enjoy the moonlight so fair,
And the shimmering stars spread everywhere;

The legendary tale of the moon being made of cheese,
And bursting of the wolf because of drinking pond water, oh jeez!!!
In the dead of chilly nights,you might feel your blood freeze,
But as long as you can see the moon,you might probably enjoy the cool breeze;

Another ancient tale,so mythic,
Of Alklha, a monster so terrific;
Who nibbles the moon bit by bit,
And then throws it up because eating the moon wasn't legit;

Mythology never fails to shock,
All these tales change with the clock;
But the sky and the ocean are eternal,
Now go back and sleep, because you aren't nocturnal.

~Sunaina

14. TEARS OF LONGING

We all have cried, right? The moment we exited our mom's womb and entered into this human-ly word, the first thing we did was to cry like hell, screaming and yelling! That seems funny somehow when I think of it now as a grown-up. But the amazing thing is that our first cry made our entire family laugh! That tear is something special. Gradually, we grow up and cry when we get injured and then comes teeny-age where we are the most dramatic and emotional and we shed tears of salt for absolutely nothing at all. But there are some tears that are not just filled with salt but also pain, that have a story hidden in them. I have one such story too. Sometimes, we fail to express the reason behind our tears. The painful ones are those which remind you of someone special, someone whose presence was very important for you. For me, my pet (a german shepherd by breed) was really very special. We called him Alex. Some friends leave us on the mid-road of our lives and go away. They choose to rest somewhere in peace but they never leave us. Although they might not breathe anymore but their heart always beats in ours. Such friends are rare and I lost mine.

Such friends can bring back happy memories from the past that can make us laugh and cry at the same time and those tears aren't 'tears of joy' , they are tears of those memories, they are the tears of the pain of not having them beside us, they are the tears of missing those happy moments with them, they are the 'TEARS OF LONGING.'

TEARS OF LONGING

Oh dear! Where have you gone?
I can feel your heart beating in mine,
In the distant universe, I can see you shine!

Oh dear! Why are you gone?
I miss those amazing days I had spent with you,
And now, you have become like the morning dew!

Oh dear! Do you know how much I yearn for you?
Those silly things we did in the past,
Fill my eyes with tears so fast,
I laugh and I cry,
I try to hold back my tears but I fail, I don't know why !

Everytime, when our memories flash in my head,
Although unwilling, innumerable tears I shed,
I grieve for you with a smile on my face,
I grive for our memories with anguish in my eyes.
I cry for our memories,
I cry longing for you.
'Tears of longing' roll down my cheeks, everytime I think of you.

~Sunaina

15. THE PROMISE

Right now, you must be wondering why I used 'THE' before the word 'PROMISE'. It's because a very dear one of mine made me understand the true meaning and value of promises. Promises have been there since ages, even religious books and other ancient books have the reference of promises in them. We the humans have somehow obliterated the value of promises and we take it very very casually and lightly. However, my loved one taught me the true meaning of this word. I would not say much about it, you will get to know the story as you go through the lines of the poem. It's true that a lot of times, we accidentally break promises ;those which others give us or the ones that we do to ourselves. It's very onerous to keep a promise till the very end but we should try at leas. I have seen many people who consider those precious promises as blagues. This should not be happening, we have got a heart along with a brain as well. As a child, I had heard that emotions are the only things that make us humans, not animals. And look at now, I feel like humans are no longer worthy of being called as humans, my pet that too a dog taught me a very important chapter of life.

Here, I share a very true story of mine, in which I have narrated how my bestest friend pulled out all the stops to keep 'THE PROMISE.'

THE PROMISE

There's one such promise in our mortal existence,
That makes us question our own conscience!

Do you think that we the mere humans are any longer worthy of being called humane?
The way we disrespect those immensely powerful promises that were once created by us is insane!

What do you think, humans?
Do you think promises are just illusions?

My bestest friend,
A dog by breed,
A part of my family,
A part of my mortal life and immortal soul.

We lived blissfully every day,
He used to pull my clothes everytime I crossed his way;
We fought with each other,
We consoled each other,

But as the rule goes- "Nothing lasts forever",
He fell sick and had a bad fever,
We thought it would be okay,
But his deteriorating health made us think the other way,
I was scared and
All I could do was to pray;
But does God listen to us everytime? -- nay!

With a sense of foreboding,
I sat beside him with my hands quivering;
I held his paw,
And looked into his eyes;
Do you know what i saw?
They had a distant look as if they were already saying goodbyes.
I asked him to promise me,
Never ever to leave me;
I call it 'THE PROMISE'

He did keep his promise till the very end,
Each other's withering soul, we were trying to mend;
I very well remember that last day,
It was a Sunday morning,
And he lay on the floor since the previous night,

The clock ticked,
And ache in my soul increased.

Somewhere in a corner of my heart,
I was still waiting for a miracle to happen,
But when I saw his eyes dampen;
I sat beside him,
With an expression so grim,
I patted him on his head,
And said,
"You can go now,I take my promise back"
And I said him goodbye with a gentle kiss on his forehead,
With his lifeless eyes; into my eyes he stared;
This is how true love keeps 'THE PROMISE.'

~Sunaina

9 798886 672183

Printed by Libri Plureos GmbH in Hamburg, Germany